T5-DHJ-503

31454 0959 4

SHERYL CROW
The Globe Sessions

Transcribed by HEMME LUTTJEBOER and DANNY BEGELMAN

Project Managers: JEANNETTE DeLISA and AARON STANG
Music Editor: COLGAN BRYAN
Book Art Layout: LISA GREENE MANE
Album Art: ©1998 A&M Records, Inc.
Album Art Direction & Design: JERI HEIDEN
Album Photography: PETER LINDBERGH, TCHAD BLAKE
Special Thanks to JUDY STAKEE

WARNER BROS. PUBLICATIONS - THE GLOBAL LEADER IN PRINT
USA: 15800 NW 48th Avenue, Miami, FL 33014

WARNER/CHAPPELL MUSIC   Carisch NUOVA CARISCH   IMP INTERNATIONAL MUSIC PUBLICATIONS LIMITED

CANADA: 40 SHEPPARD AVE. WEST, SUITE 800
TORONTO, ONTARIO, M2N 6K9
SCANDINAVIA: P.O. BOX 533 VENDEVAGEN 85 B
S-182 15, DANDERYD, SWEDEN
AUSTRALIA: P.O. BOX 353
3 TALAVERA ROAD, NORTH RYDE N.S.W. 2113

ITALY: VIA CAMPANIA, 12
20098 S. GIULIANO MILANESE (MI)
ZONA INDUSTRIALE SESTO ULTERIANO
SPAIN: MAGALLANES, 25
28015 MADRID
FRANCE: 25 RUE DE L'AUTEVILLE, 75010 PARIS

ENGLAND: SOUTHEND ROAD
WOODFORD GREEN, ESSEX IG8 8HN
GERMANY: MARSTALLSTR. 8, D-80539 MÜNCHEN
DENMARK: DANMUSIK, VOGNMAGERGADE 7
DK-1120 KØBENHAVN K

© 1998 WARNER BROS. PUBLICATIONS
All Rights Reserved

Any duplication, adaptation or arrangement of the compositions
contained in this collection requires the written consent of the Publisher.
No part of this book may be photocopied or reproduced in any way without permission.
Unauthorized uses are an infringement of the U.S. Copyright Act and are punishable by law.

Contents

The Globe Sessions.

MY FAVORITE MISTAKE

Words and Music by
SHERYL CROW and JEFF TROTT

Moderate rock ♩ = 104

Intro:
Band tacet

© 1998 WARNER-TAMERLANE PUBLISHING CORP., OLD CROW MUSIC and TROTTSKY MUSIC
All Rights on behalf of OLD CROW MUSIC Administered by WARNER-TAMERLANE PUBLISHING CORP.
All Rights on behalf of TROTTSKY MUSIC Administered by WIXEN MUSIC PUBLISHING, INC.
All Rights Reserved

8

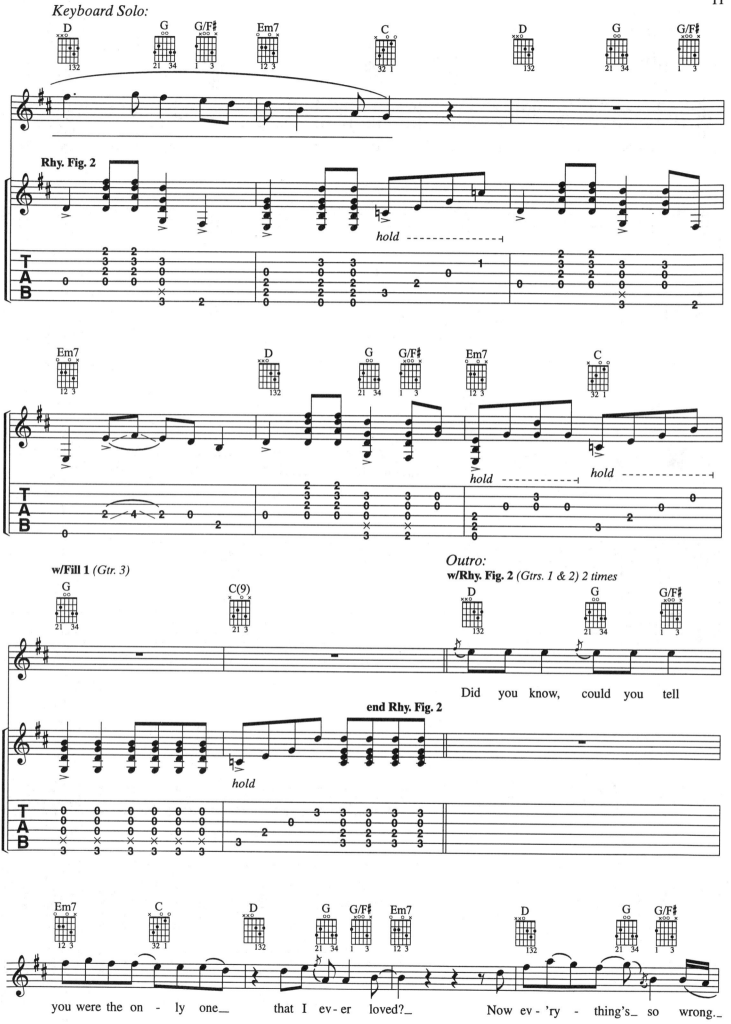

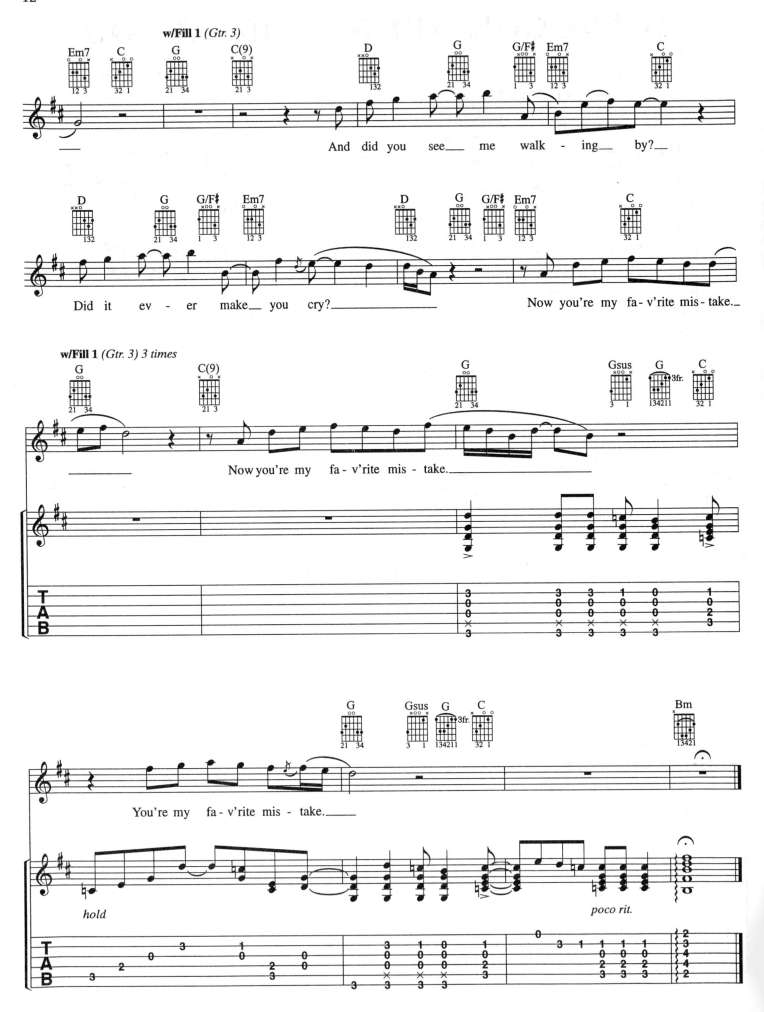

THERE GOES THE NEIGHBORHOOD

Words and Music by
SHERYL CROW and JEFF TROTT

*All pitches sound 1/2 step higher than written. Tab numbers are relative to capo position.

There Goes the Neighborhood - 7 - 1
0319B

© 1998 WARNER-TAMERLANE PUBLISHING CORP., OLD CROW MUSIC and TROTTSKY MUSIC
All Rights on behalf of OLD CROW MUSIC Administered by WARNER-TAMERLANE PUBLISHING CORP.
All Rights on behalf of TROTTSKY MUSIC Administered by WIXEN MUSIC PUBLISHING, INC.
All Rights Reserved

*Two gtrs. arr. for one gtr.

And Cow-boy Jane's in bed,_____
And School-boy John's in jail,_____

nurs-ing a swol-len head._____
mak-ing a kill-ing through the U. S. Mail.

Sun-shine Sal-ly and Pe-

Chorus:
w/Fill 1 (Horns)

Rhy. Fig. 2

Fill 1

Horns

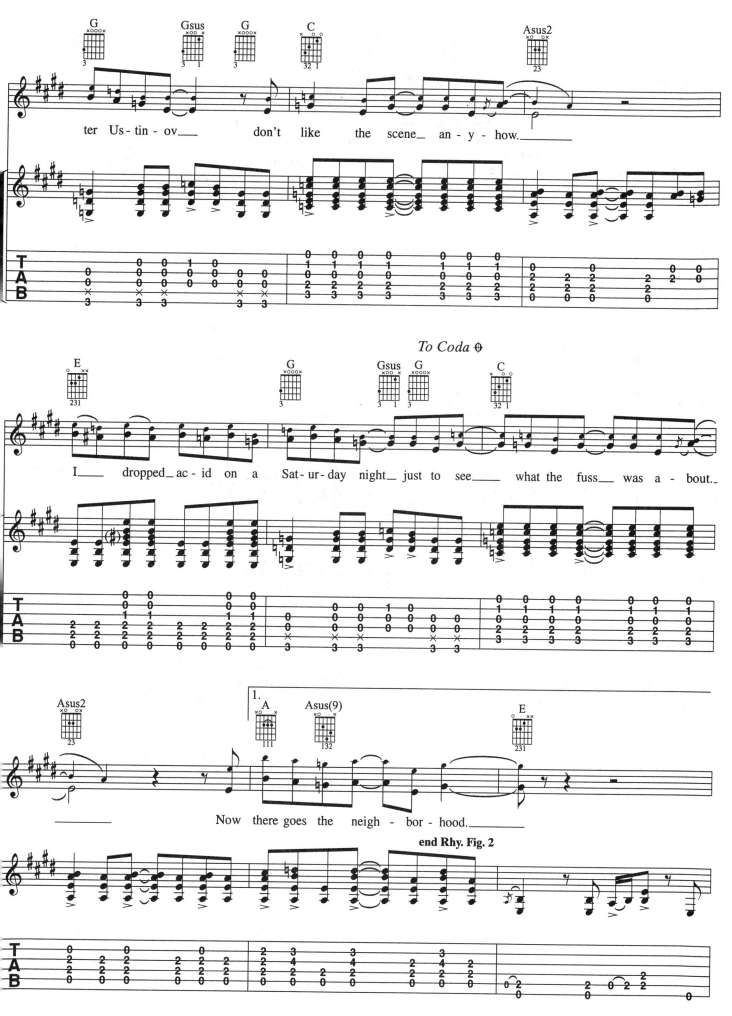

ter Us - tin - ov___ don't like the scene___ an - y - how.___

To Coda ✆

I___ dropped___ac - id on a Sat - ur - day night___ just to see___ what the fuss___ was a - bout.

Now there goes the neigh - bor - hood.___

end Rhy. Fig. 2

Verse 3:
w/Rhy. Fig. 1 (Gtr. 1) 2 times

- ie of the screen - play of the book__ a - bout__ a girl__ who meets a junk - ie.__

The mes - sen - ger gets shot down just for car - ry - ing__ the mes - sage to a

flunk - ie.__ We can't be cer - tain who the vil - lains are__ 'cuz ev - 'ry - one's__ so

pret - ty.__ But the af - ter par - ty's sure to be__ a wing-

D.S. 𝄋 al Coda

- ding, as it moves in - to your____ cit - y.__ Oh.__

There Goes the Neighborhood - 7 - 5
0319B

18

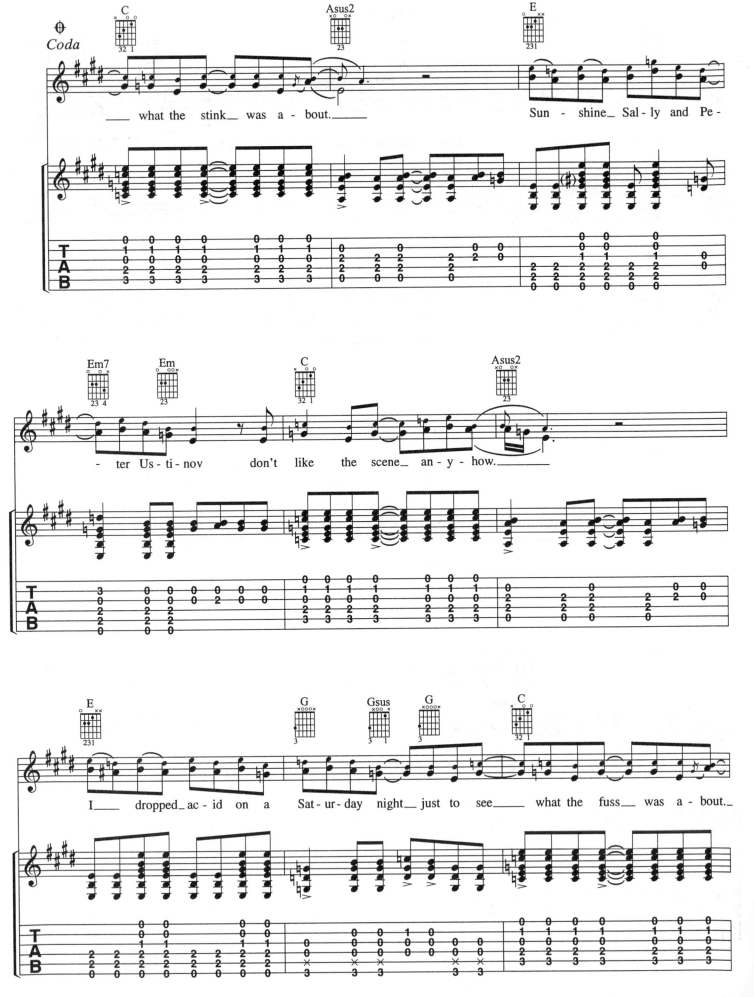

*Primary vocal doubled 8va.

*Vocal doubled 8va.

RIVERWIDE

Words and Music by
SHERYL CROW

Gtr. 1 tuned to "Open B":

⑥ = B ③ = F♯
⑤ = F♯ ② = B
④ = B ① = D♯

Gtr. 2 is in standard tuning

Moderately ♩ = 102 ($\frac{12}{8}$ feel ♫ = ♩♪)

Intro:

B5

Gtr. 1 *(Acoustic, "Open B" tuning)*

mf w/thumb and fingers
hold throughout

Gtr. 2 *(Electric, standard tuning)*

w/flanger & vibrato effects

Riverwide - 9 - 1
0319B

© 1998 WARNER-TAMERLANE PUBLISHING CORP. and OLD CROW MUSIC
All Rights Administered by WARNER-TAMERLANE PUBLISHING CORP.
All Rights Reserved

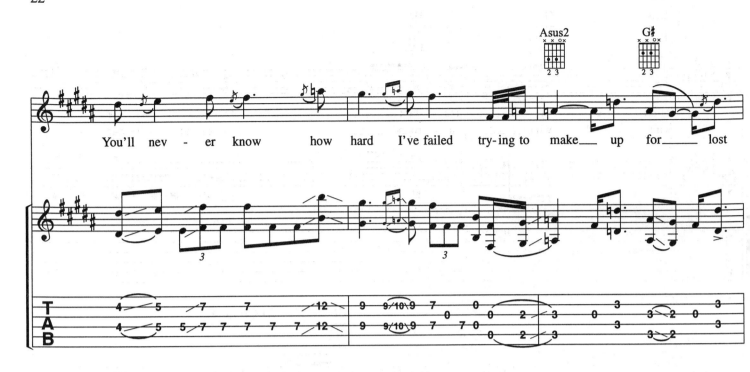

You'll nev - er know how hard I've failed try-ing to make___ up for___ lost

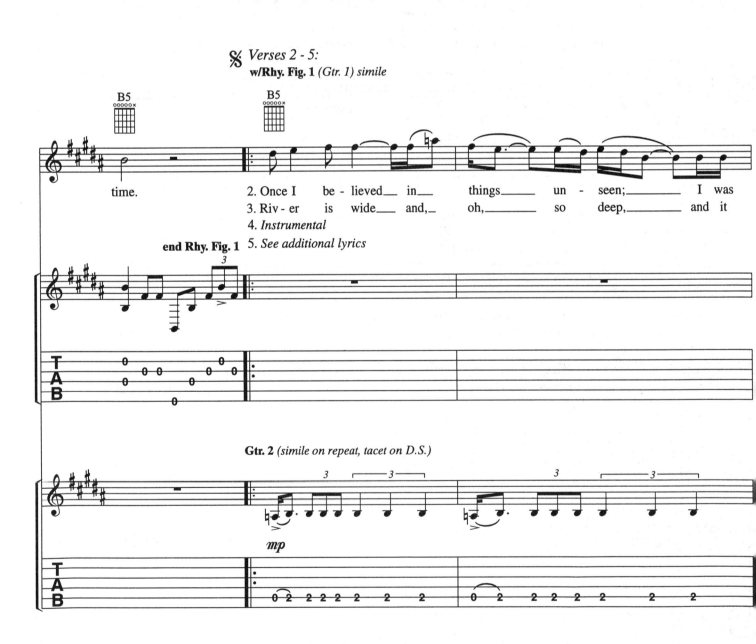

time.

2. Once I be - lieved___ in___ things___ un - seen;___ I was
3. Riv - er is wide___ and,___ oh,___ so deep,___ and it
4. *Instrumental*
5. *See additional lyrics*

end Rhy. Fig. 1

Gtr. 2 (*simile on repeat, tacet on D.S.*)

mp

24

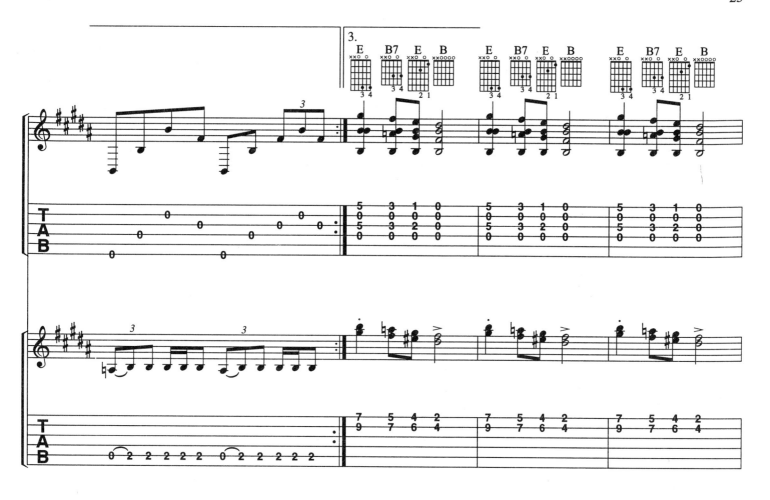

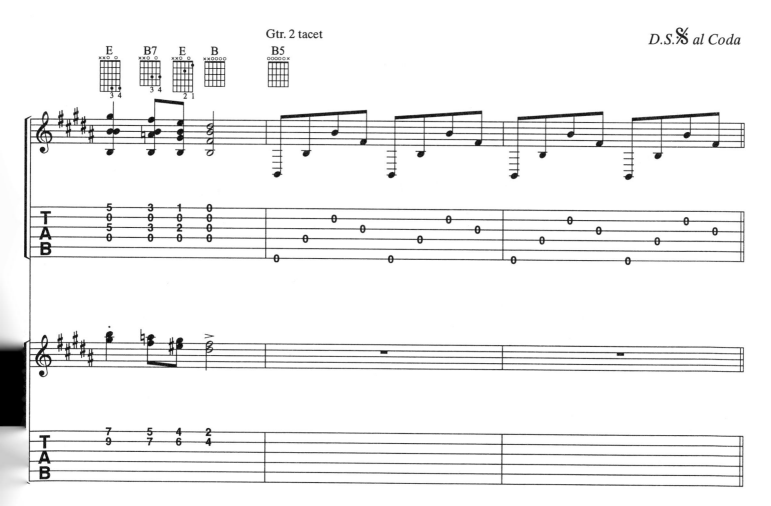

Verse 5:
Tell ma I loved the man,
Even though I turned and ran.
Lovely and fine, I could have been
Laying down in the palm of his hand.

MAYBE THAT'S SOMETHING

Words and Music by
SHERYL CROW and JEFF TROTT

All gtrs. tune down 1/2 step

Moderately ♩ = 92

Intro:

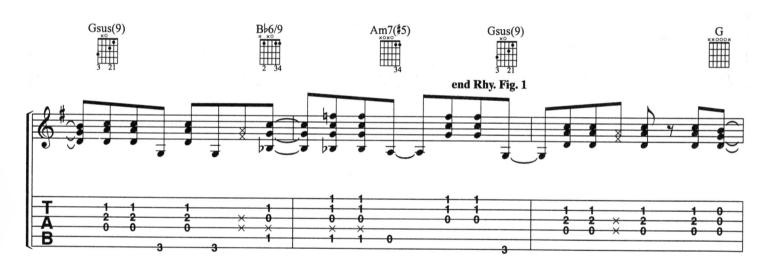

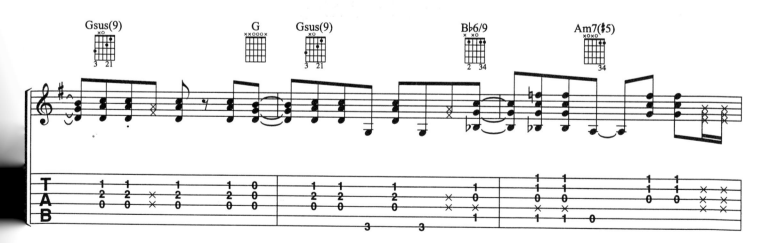

Maybe That's Something - 9 - 1
0319B

© 1998 WARNER-TAMERLANE PUBLISHING CORP., OLD CROW MUSIC and TROTTSKY MUSIC
All Rights on behalf of OLD CROW MUSIC Administered by WARNER-TAMERLANE PUBLISHING CORP.
All Rights on behalf of TROTTSKY MUSIC Administered by WIXEN MUSIC PUBLISHING, INC.
All Rights Reserved

30

IT DON'T HURT

Words and Music by
SHERYL CROW and JEFF TROTT

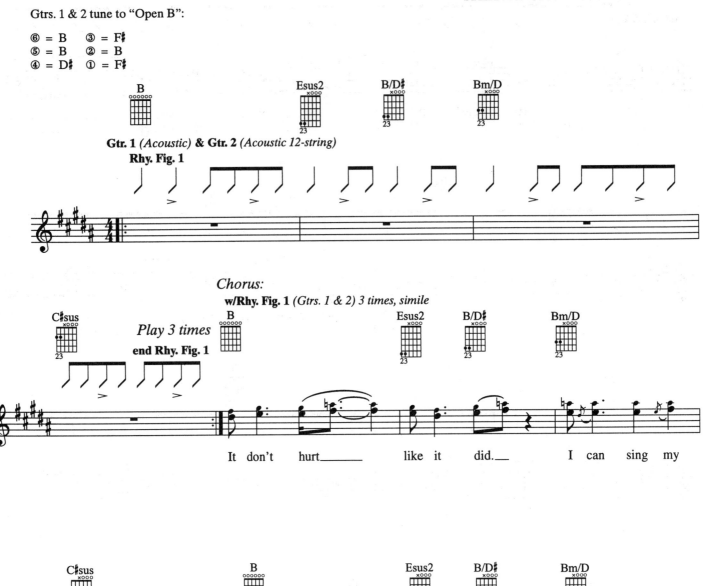

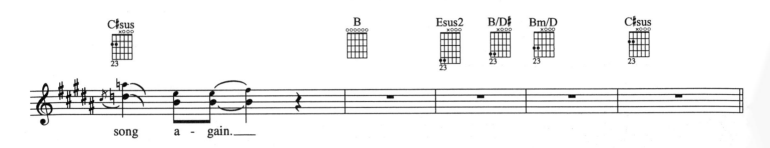

It Don't Hurt - 8 - 1
0319B

© 1998 WARNER-TAMERLANE PUBLISHING CORP., OLD CROW MUSIC and TROTTSKY MUSIC
All Rights on behalf of OLD CROW MUSIC Administered by WARNER-TAMERLANE PUBLISHING CORP.
All Rights on behalf of TROTTSKY MUSIC Administered by WIXEN MUSIC PUBLISHING, INC.
All Rights Reserved

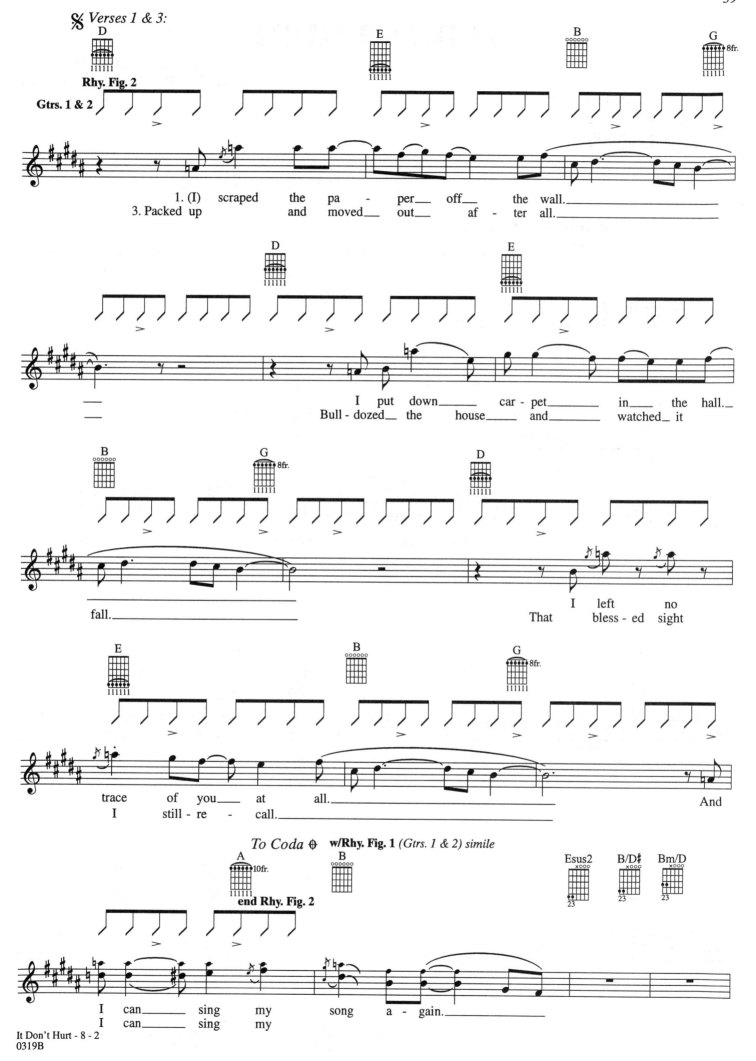

It Don't Hurt - 8 - 4
0319B

42

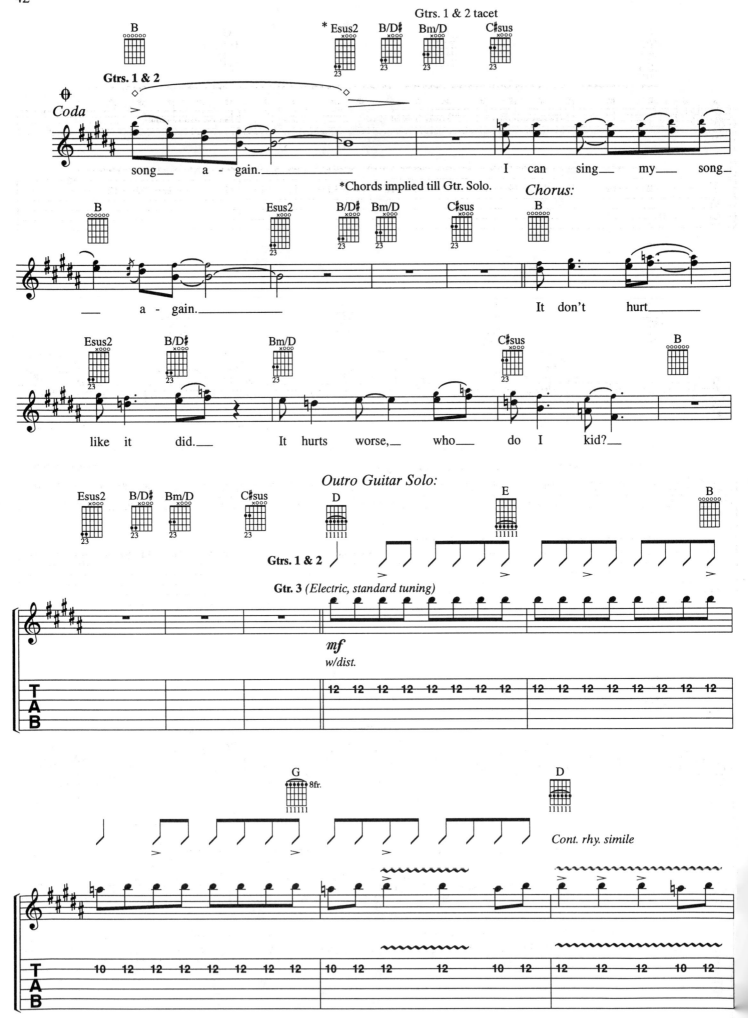

It Don't Hurt - 8 - 5
0319B

44

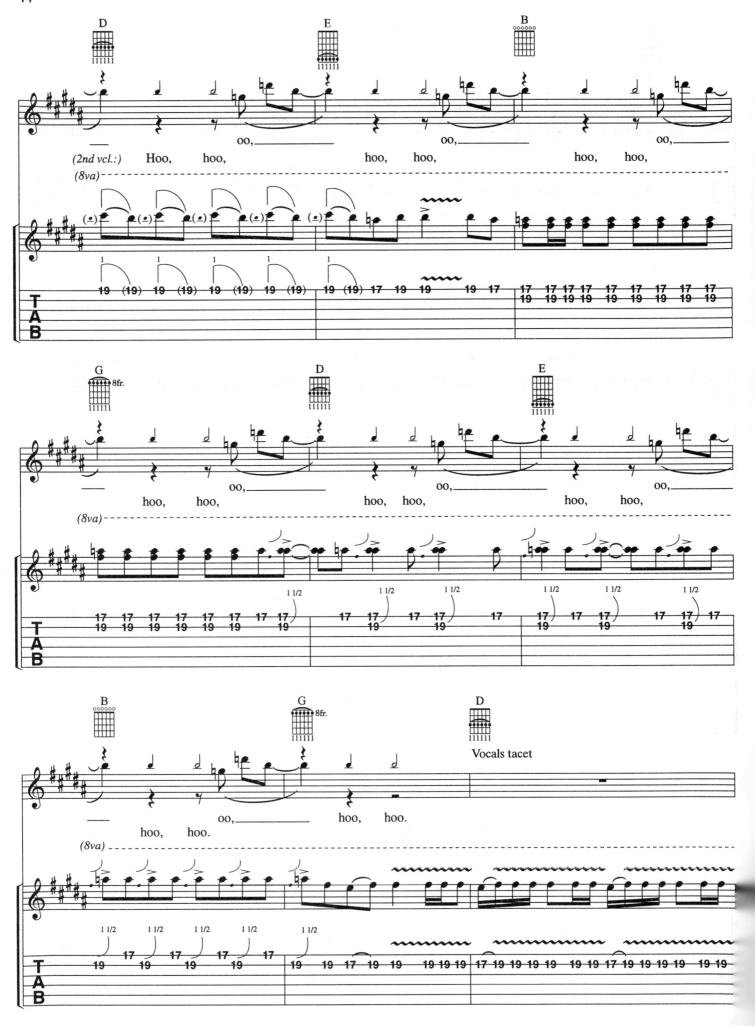

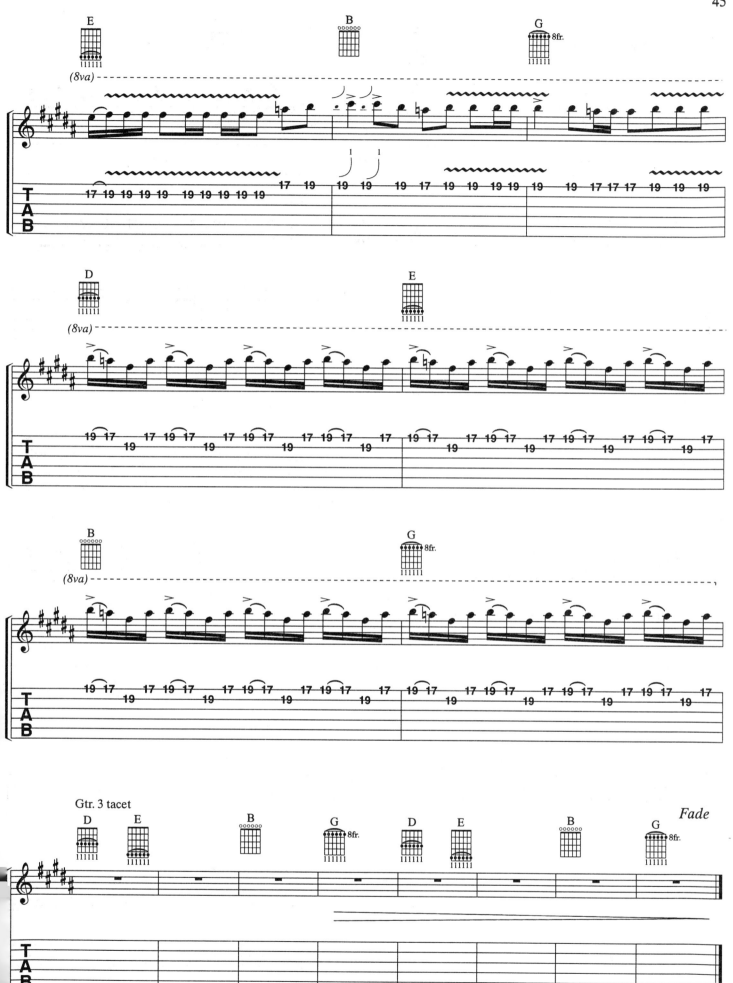

AM I GETTING THROUGH
(Part 1 & 2)

Words and Music by
SHERYL CROW

Am I Getting Through - 9 - 1
0319B

© 1998 WARNER-TAMERLANE PUBLISHING CORP. and OLD CROW MUSIC
All Rights Administered by WARNER-TAMERLANE PUBLISHING CORP.
All Rights Reserved

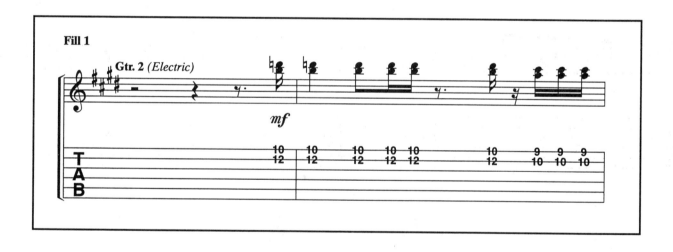

48

*Chord is implied by strings.

Part 2

THE DIFFICULT KIND

Words and Music by
SHERYL CROW

© 1998 WARNER-TAMERLANE PUBLISHING CORP. and OLD CROW MUSIC
All Rights Administered by WARNER-TAMERLANE PUBLISHING CORP.
All Rights Reserved

58

The Difficult Kind - 7 - 4
0319B

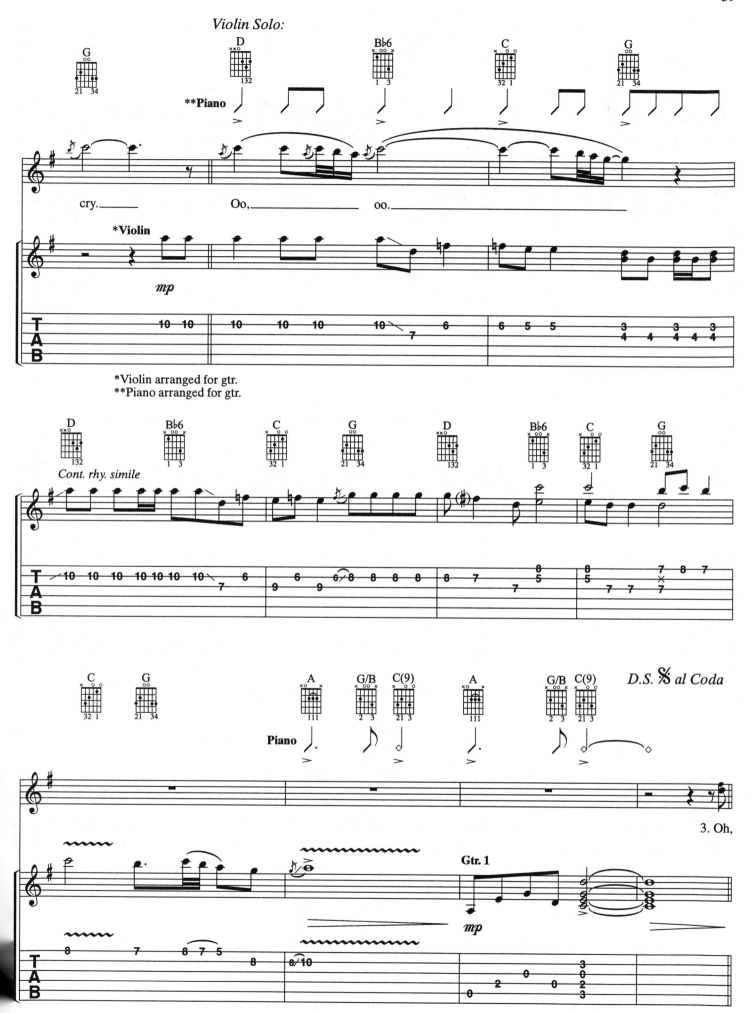

Verse 3:
Oh, ballbreaking moon and ridiculing stars,
The older I get, the closer you are.
Don't you have somewhere you need to be,
Instead of hanging here, making a fool of me?
(To Chorus:)

ANYTHING BUT DOWN

Words and Music by
SHERYL CROW

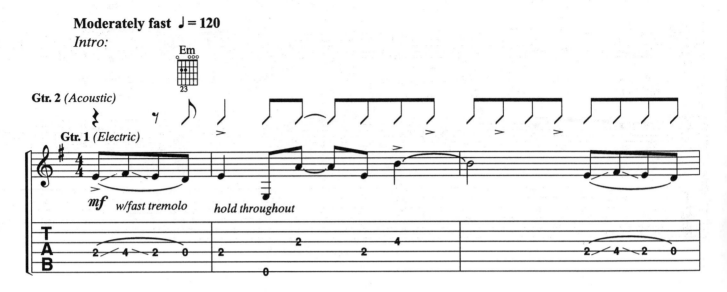

© 1998 WARNER-TAMERLANE PUBLISHING CORP. and OLD CROW MUSIC
All Rights Administered by WARNER-TAMERLANE PUBLISHING CORP.
All Rights Reserved

64

Chorus:

But you don't bring me an - y - thing___ but down.___

*Rhy. Fig. 1

*Composite arrangement of two gtrs.

w/Rhy. Fig. 1 (Gtr. 1) 2 times, simile

Cont. rhy. simile

No, you don't bring me an -

end Rhy. Fig. 1

To Coda ⊕

- y - thing___ but down.___

You don't bring me an -

- y - thing___ but down___

when you come___ a - round.___

66

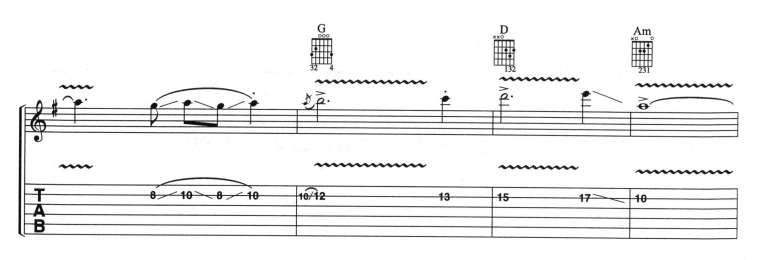

D.S. 𝄋 *al Coda*

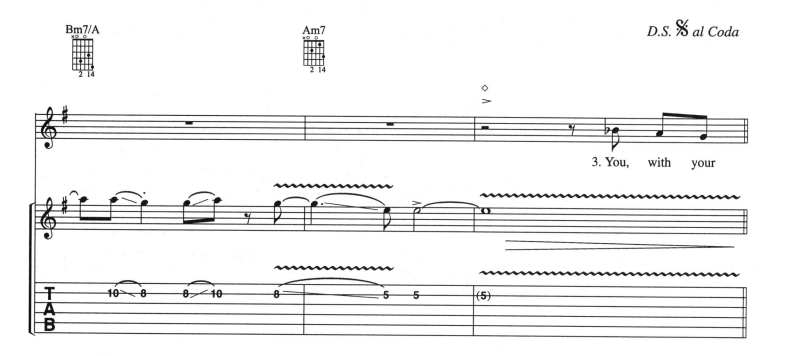

3. You, with your

Now, ev-'ry-thing just crash-es to___ the ground.___

Lyrics: when you came a-round,

when you come a-round.

Well,

Outro:

Verse 3:
You, with your silky words.
You, with your eyes of green and blue.
You, with your steel beliefs
That don't match anything you do.
It was so much easier before you became you.
(To Chorus:)

MISSISSIPPI

Words and Music by
BOB DYLAN

Moderately fast ♩ = 122

Intro:

Mississippi - 7 - 1
0319B

© 1997 SPECIAL RIDER MUSIC (SESAC)
This Arrangement © 1998 SPECIAL RIDER MUSIC (SESAC)
All Rights Reserved   Used by Permission of Music Sales Corporation

Outro:
w/Lead Fig. 1 *(Keybd.)* simile

Play 3 times & fade

Verse 3:
Devil's in the alley, mule kicking in the stall.
Say anything you want to, I've heard it all.
I was thinking about things that she said.
I was dreaming I was sleeping in your bed.

Verse 4:
Walking through the leaves, falling from the trees.
Feel like a stranger who nobody sees.
So many things we never will undo.
I know you're sorry, but I'm sorry too.
(To Pre-chorus 2:)

Verse 5:
Well, my ship's been split to splinters, it's sinking fast.
I'm drowning in the poison, got no future, got no past.
But my, my heart's not beating, its mind is free.
I got nothing but affection for those who sail with me.

Verse 6:
Everybody's moving, they ain't already there.
Everybody's got to move somewhere.
Well, stick with me, baby, anyhow.
Things should start to get interesting right about now.

Pre-chorus 3:
Well, my clothes are wet,
They're tight on my skin.
Not as tight as the corner that I painted myself in.
I know that fortune is waiting to be kind,
So give me your hand
And say you'll be mine.

Chorus 3:
The evidence is endless,
You're going astray.
You can always come back,
But you can't come back all away.
(To Coda)

CRASH AND BURN

Words and Music by
SHERYL CROW

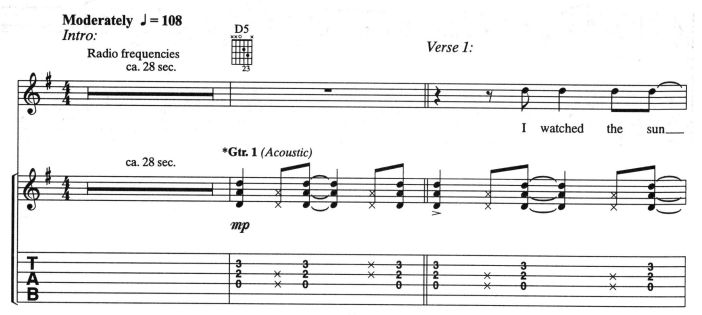

*Gtr. 1 and vocals sound a 4th higher than notated.
**Tap strings lightly with right-hand fingers.

© 1998 WARNER-TAMERLANE PUBLISHING CORP. and OLD CROW MUSIC
All Rights Administered by WARNER-TAMERLANE PUBLISHING CORP.
All Rights Reserved

82

Crash and Burn - 13 - 6
0319B

Crash and Burn - 13 - 9
0319B

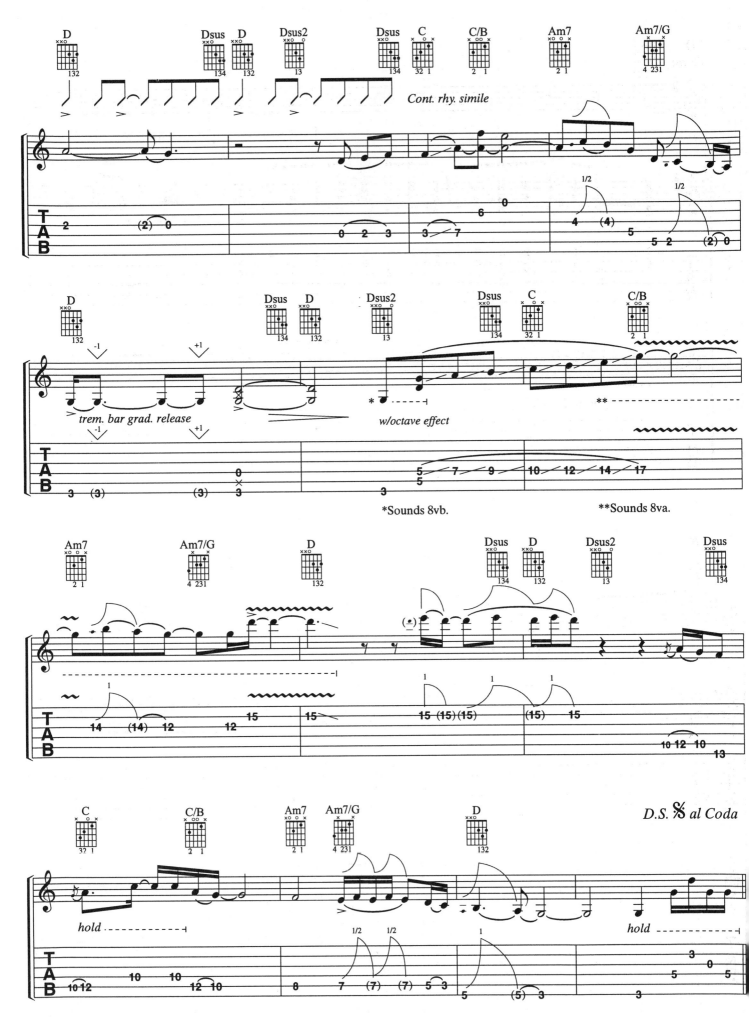

Outro:

To the crash and burn,_____

mf hold - *rake*

burn._____

Cont. simile

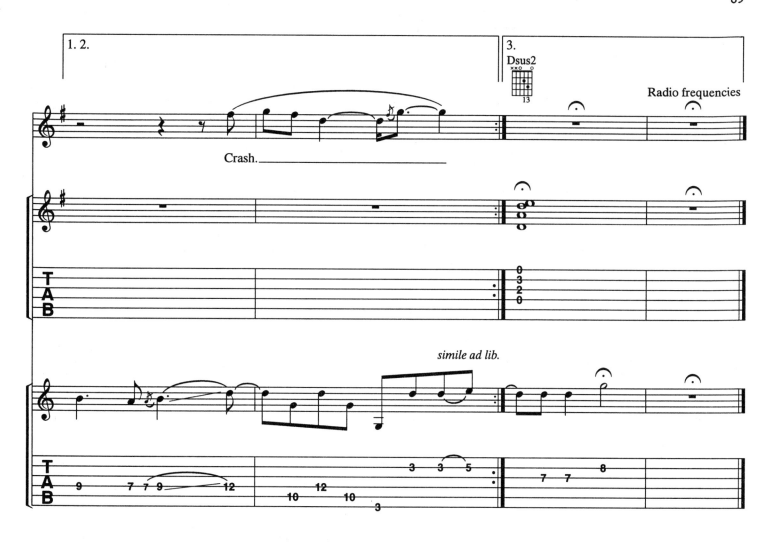

Verse 4:
Antigone laid across the road
And let a Mac truck leave her there for dead
Just because her lover split the scene.
Well, love may be great, but why lose your head?

Chorus 3:
Well, it's laughter that comes out when I cry for you,
And my heart may break again before it learns;
And I might be stupid enough to want to fall again
'Cause I've gotten used
To crash and burn.
(To Outro:)

MEMBERS ONLY

Words and Music by
SHERYL CROW

All gtrs. tune down 1/2 step:

⑥ = E♭   ③ = G♭
⑤ = A♭   ② = B♭
④ = D♭   ① = E♭

Moderately fast ♩ = 120
Intro:

Gtr. 2 (Acoustic)

w/pick and fingers

Gtr. 3 (Electric) on 3rd time only

mf w/dist.

© 1998 WARNER-TAMERLANE PUBLISHING CORP. and OLD CROW MUSIC
All Rights Administered by WARNER-TAMERLANE PUBLISHING CORP.
All Rights Reserved

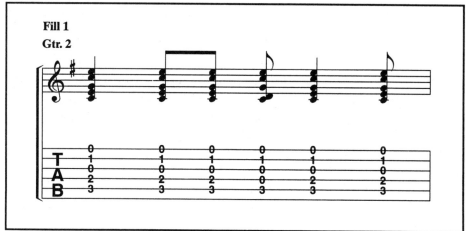

94

in mar - ti - ni glass - es

with black - strap mo - las - ses

'cause I can't take it an - y - more.

'cause I can't taste it an - y - more.

Gtr. 1 (dbld.)

w/Fill 2 (Gtr. 2)

Cont. rhy. simile

No, 'cause I can't taste it an-y-more.

Interlude:
w/Rhy. Fig. 1 *(Gtr. 2) simile*

Gtr. 1 *(dbld.)*

To Coda ⊕

Guitar Solo:

Gtrs. 1 & 2

Gtr. 3 *(dist.)*

Gtr. 1

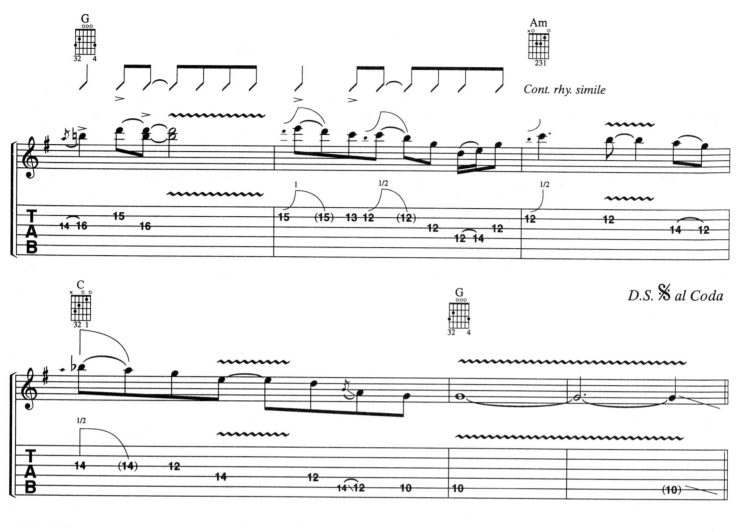

D.S. % al Coda

Verse 3:
My friend Gregg says it's all good,
As the eastern seaboard's blown away.
Now everything is going half-priced,
So look at all the money we saved.

Chorus 3:
And all the politicians shake their asses,
Looking for the back door.
Well, I'll just be hanging out with the lasses
'Cause they don't like the boys no more.
No, and I can't take it anymore.

SUBWAY RIDE

Words and Music by
SHERYL CROW

Moderately ♩ = 86

Intro:

Do, do,＿ do, do. Do, do,＿ do, do. Do, do,＿ do, do.

*Implied harmony.

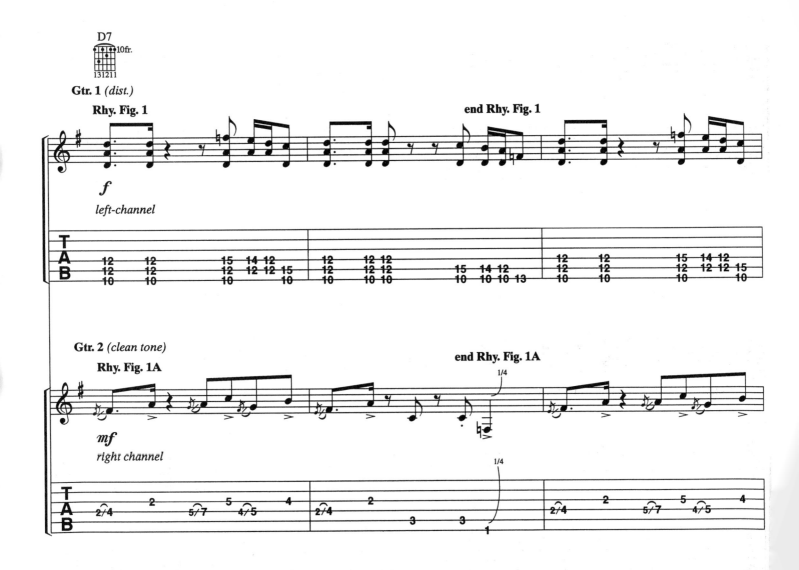

© 1998 WARNER-TAMERLANE PUBLISHING CORP. and OLD CROW MUSIC
All Rights Administered by WARNER-TAMERLANE PUBLISHING CORP.
All Rights Reserved

To Coda ⊕ **w/Rhy. Figs. 1** *(Gtr. 1)* **& 1A** *(Gtr. 2) 3 times, simile*

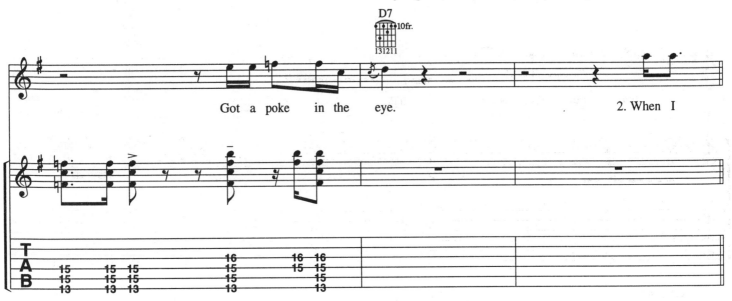

Got a poke   in the   eye.   2. When I

Verses 2 & 4:

read the lat - est news,__ how we can't be - lieve__ he wore__ those   shoes.__   Should we
4. *See additional lyrics*

have the man__   im - peached or should we   shoot him   in   the   foot?__ Well, you waste my

time.____   You   waste   my   time____   look - ing   for

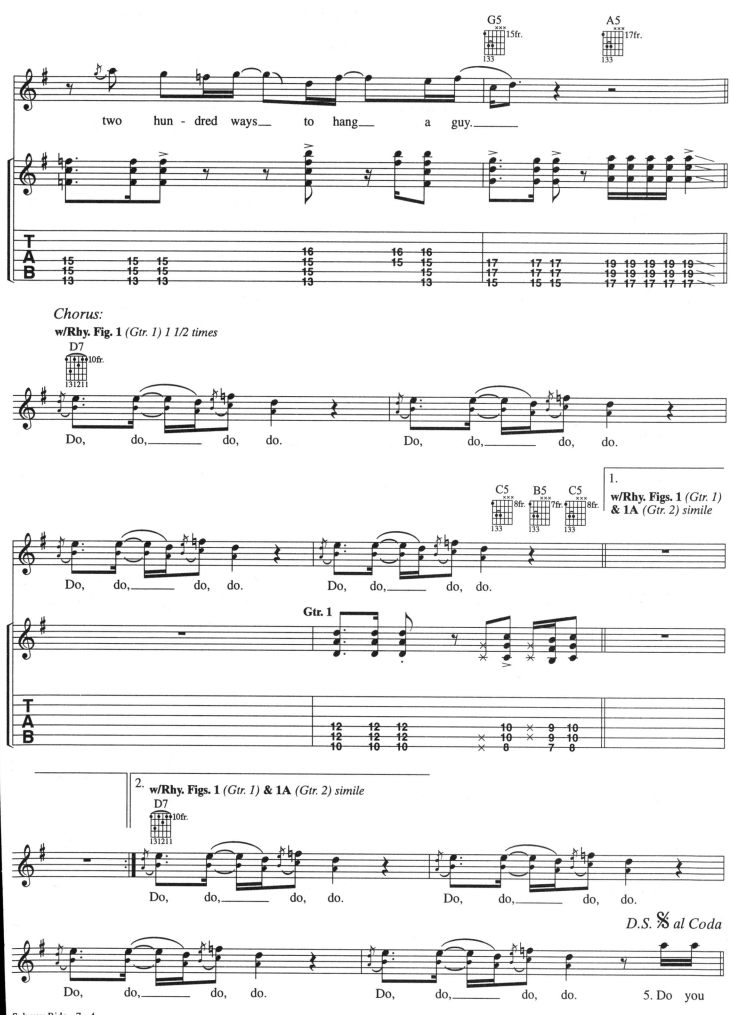

Verse 6:

w/Rhy. Figs. 1 *(Gtr. 1)* **& 1A** *(Gtr. 2) 2 times, simile*

Wait and see,__ the boom_ will fall,__ the morn-ing eggs_ will hit_ the wall._ And

ev-'ry-one__ I know_ will call__ to say that change is hang-ing in the air._

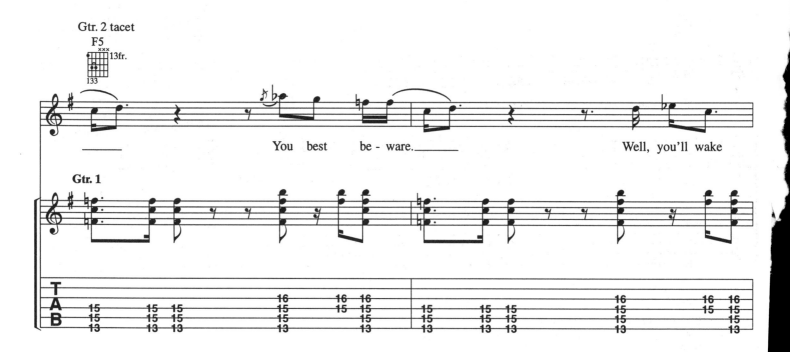

_____ You best be-ware._____ Well, you'll wake

up and av-'rage Joe__ is in__ your chair.___ Just be-cause_

Start slow fade

Do, do,_____ do, do. Do, do,_____ do, do.

I was

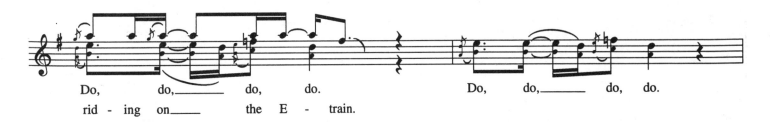

Do, do,_____ do, do. Do, do,_____ do, do.

rid - ing on____ the E - train.

Do, do,_____ do, do. Do, do,_____ do, do.

Fade

Do, do,_____ do, do. Do, do,_____ do, do.

Verse 3:
Allegations,
Interrogations,
Investigations,
Then more taxation.
National pastime is aggravation.
I think I'll move out to a desert isle
Just for a while.

Verse 4:
To avoid
All that's distracting,
Like newspapers and magazines,
Insipid propagandizing
To tell me what a loser I've elected.
But you've neglected to tell the truth;
That your politics is tied around his foot
And we, too, are dangling.

Verse 5:
Do you think that we are crazy,
Low I.Q., that we are lazy,
That we sit here watching sitcoms,
That we have no clue to what is going on?
You've got that wrong.

GUITAR TAB GLOSSARY **

TABLATURE EXPLANATION

READING TABLATURE: Tablature illustrates the six strings of the guitar. Notes and chords are indicated by the placement of fret numbers on a given string(s).

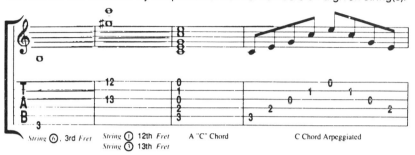

String ⑥, 3rd Fret String ① 12th Fret A "C" Chord   C Chord Arpeggiated
String ① 13th Fret

BENDING NOTES

HALF STEP: Play the note and bend string one half step.*

SLIGHT BEND (Microtone): Play the note and bend string slightly to the equivalent of half a fret.

WHOLE STEP: Play the note and bend string one whole step.

PREBEND (Ghost Bend): Bend to the specified note, before the string is picked.

WHOLE STEP AND A HALF: Play the note and bend string a whole step and a half.

PREBEND AND RELEASE: Bend the string, play it, then release to the original note.

TWO STEPS: Play the note and bend string two whole steps.

REVERSE BEND: Play the already-bent string, then immediately drop it down to the fretted note.

BEND AND RELEASE: Play the note and gradually bend to the next pitch, then release to the original note. Only the first note is attacked.

BENDS INVOLVING MORE THAN ONE STRING: Play the note and bend string while playing an additional note (or notes) on another string(s). Upon release, relieve pressure from additional note(s), causing original note to sound alone.

BENDS INVOLVING STATIONARY NOTES: Play notes and bend lower pitch, then hold until release begins (indicated at the point where line becomes solid).

UNISON BEND: Play both notes and immediately bend the lower note to the same pitch as the higher note.

DOUBLE NOTE BEND: Play both notes and immediately bend both strings simultaneously.

*A half step is the smallest interval in Western music; it is equal to one fret. A whole step equals two frets.

© 1990 Beam Me Up Music
c/o CPP/Belwin, Inc. Miami, Florida 33014
International Copyright Secured   Made in U.S.A.   All Rights Reserved   **By Kenn Chipkin and Aaron Stang

RHYTHM SLASHES

STRUM INDICATIONS: Strum with indicated rhythm.

The chord voicings are found on the first page of the transcription underneath the song title.

INDICATING SINGLE NOTES USING RHYTHM SLASHES: Very often single notes are incorporated into a rhythm part. The note name is indicated above the rhythm slash with a fret number and a string indication.

ARTICULATIONS

HAMMER ON: Play lower note, then "hammer on" to higher note with another finger. Only the first note is attacked.

LEFT HAND HAMMER: Hammer on the first note played on each string with the left hand.

PULL OFF: Play higher note, then "pull off" to lower note with another finger. Only the first note is attacked.

FRETBOARD TAPPING: "Tap" onto the note indicated by + with a finger of the pick hand, then pull off to the following note held by the fret hand.

TAP SLIDE: Same as fretboard tapping, but the tapped note is slid randomly up the fretboard, then pulled off to the following note.

BEND AND TAP TECHNIQUE: Play note and bend to specified interval. While holding bend, tap onto note indicated.

LEGATO SLIDE: Play note and slide to the following note. (Only first note is attacked).

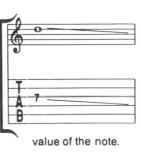

LONG GLISSANDO: Play note and slide in specified direction for the full value of the note.

SHORT GLISSANDO: Play note for its full value and slide in specified direction at the last possible moment.

PICK SLIDE: Slide the edge of the pick in specified direction across the length of the string(s).

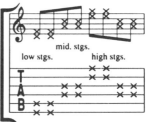

MUTED STRINGS: A percussive sound is made by laying the fret hand across all six strings while pick hand strikes specified area (low, mid, high strings).

PALM MUTE: The note or notes are muted by the palm of the pick hand by lightly touching the string(s) near the bridge.

TREMOLO PICKING: The note or notes are picked as fast as possible.

TRILL: Hammer on and pull off consecutively and as fast as possible between the original note and the grace note.

ACCENT: Notes or chords are to be played with added emphasis.

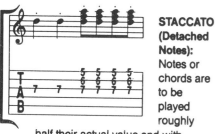

STACCATO (Detached Notes): Notes or chords are to be played roughly half their actual value and with separation.

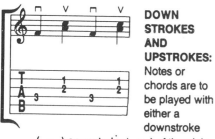
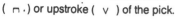

DOWN STROKES AND UPSTROKES: Notes or chords are to be played with either a downstroke (⊓ ▪) or upstroke (∨) of the pick.

VIBRATO: The pitch of a note is varied by a rapid shaking of the fret hand finger, wrist, and forearm.

HARMONICS

NATURAL HARMONIC: A finger of the fret hand lightly touches the note or notes indicated in the tab and is played by the pick hand.

ARTIFICIAL HARMONIC: The first tab number is fretted, then the pick hand produces the harmonic by using a finger to lightly touch the same string at the second tab number (in parenthesis) and is then picked by another finger.

ARTIFICIAL "PINCH" HARMONIC: A note is fretted as indicated by the tab, then the pick hand produces the harmonic by squeezing the pick firmly while using the tip of the index finger in the pick attack. If parenthesis are found around the fretted note, it does not sound. No parenthesis means both the fretted note and A.H. are heard simultaneously.

TREMOLO BAR

SPECIFIED INTERVAL: The pitch of a note or chord is lowered to a specified interval and then may or may not return to the original pitch. The activity of the tremolo bar is graphically represented by peaks and valleys.

UN-SPECIFIED INTERVAL: The pitch of a note or a chord is lowered to an unspecified interval.